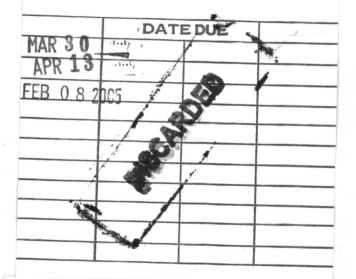

DNA

DNA
THE THREAD OF LIFE

Frank H. Wilcox

Lerner Publications Company **Minneapolis**

*To my wife, Jean, my daughter,
Susan, and my son, Bruce*

Library of Congress Cataloging-in-Publication Data

Wilcox, Frank H.
    DNA: the thread of life/by Frank H. Wilcox.
      p.   cm.
    Includes index.
    Summary: Presents the most recent information on the way
in which DNA controls the operations of cells, using models and
comparisons to familiar information systems.
    ISBN 0-8225-1584-9 (lib. bdg.)
    1. DNA—Juvenile literature. 2. Genetics—Juvenile literature.
[1. DNA. 2. Genetics.]   I. Title.
QP624.W55   1988
574.87'3282—dc19   87-31680
                                                    CIP
Manufactured in the United States of America   AC

1 2 3 4 5 6 7 8 9 10 97 96 95 94 93 92 91 90 89 88

CONTENTS

Just as a personal computer stores large amounts of information in a small space, the DNA in our cells stores all the complex information necessary for life.

INTRODUCTION

The storage of a large amount of information in a small space is becoming more and more common in our world. Whole newspapers are condensed onto small bits of microfilm. Volumes of data are stored in tiny microchips. Not very many years ago, a computer occupied a large room, but now one will fit on the top of a small desk.

This kind of storage of large amounts of information is not at all new. In each of the many cells that make up our bodies, we have information stored in the form of **DNA**. This information directs the operation of all the complex functions of the body. It also controls the formation of new cells and of new living beings, starting from a single cell. Differences in the information stored in DNA are responsible for the inherited differences among people, such as those of height, facial appearance, and skin color.

Each cell in the body has the means of packaging and storing the information of DNA in a small space. The cell can use some or all of the information, depending on its needs, and can make accurate copies of the DNA to pass the information on to new cells. The cell even has what amounts to its own word processor to correct mistakes made in copying DNA.

Genetics is the science that studies the information of life contained in DNA. Many of our early ideas about genetics came from experiments in crossbreeding animals and plants that were different from each other, such as plants with red or white flowers or animals with long or short hair. Only recently, however, have we gained a real understanding of genetics. And we are constantly learning more, thanks to important new techniques that involve a special type of DNA called **recombinant DNA.** In this book, you will learn about our newly gained knowledge of just what genetic information is, how it is used, and how it can be changed.

1
WHAT IS DNA?

You have just learned that the genetic information in cells is contained in DNA. But what is DNA? What is it made of? And, more important, what is it about DNA that provides the cell with information? This chapter will present some answers to these basic questions.

DNA is a chemical substance with a rather complex structure, but fortunately we can understand its makeup without chemical formulas or a lot of scientific jargon. A piece of DNA is like a miniature ladder,

with two sides and rungs connecting the sides. The sides of the DNA ladder are twisted around each

other, as in a spiral staircase,

with 10 rungs for each turn.

This tells us something about the shape of DNA, but we need to know more in order to learn about the information that DNA contains. We need to know what DNA is made of. It consists of three substances that are connected together in a very orderly manner. One of these is **phosphate (P)**, a chemical similar to phosphoric acid. Another is a sugar called **deoxyribose (D)**, a smaller version of the sugar glucose. The third substance is a **base**. Four different bases are present in DNA, each with a different shape. The four bases are **adenine (A)**, **cytosine (C)**, **guanine (G)**, and **thymine (T)**.

The way in which these three substances are arranged is very important to the function of DNA. It will be easier to understand this arrangement if we look at a section of DNA that is not twisted and use letters for the different parts. Still thinking of DNA as a ladder, we can say that each side piece of the ladder is a strand that is formed by units of phosphate joined with units of deoxyribose. The units alternate with each other, like this:

P - D - P - D - P - D - P - D - P - D - P - D - P - D - P - D -

The two side pieces or strands of DNA are connected by pairs of bases, which are therefore equivalent to the rungs in a ladder. When the side and the bases are combined, the DNA looks like this:

```
P - D - P - D - P - D - P - D -   P - D - P - D - P - D - P - D -
    |       |       |       |         |       |       |       |
    A       T       C       G         A       G       T       T
   ..      ..      ...     ...        ..      ...     ..      ..
    T       A       G       C         T       C       A       A
    |       |       |       |         |       |       |       |
P - D - P - D - P - D - P - D -   P - D - P - D - P - D - P - D -
```

This diagram shows only a small section of DNA. Each strand is typically much longer, and in fact, the deoxyriboses, phosphates, and bases number in the millions.

What we have described so far tells us how we get the name DNA. It is an abbreviation of **deoxyribonucleic acid**. The first part of this (deoxyribo-) comes from the type of sugar in DNA, deoxyribose, and the last part (acid) comes from the presence of phosphoric acid. The rest of the name (-nucleic) refers to the fact that DNA is found in a part of the cell called the nucleus.

Picturing DNA as a ladder is useful, but there is one way in which it is very different from a ladder. The two chains or strands in a piece of DNA can come apart from each other fairly easily. In this respect, DNA is more like a zipper. For example, the strands will separate if we merely heat DNA to nearly the temperature at which water boils. Then the DNA would look like this:

```
P - D - P - D - P - D - P - D -   P - D - P - D - P - D - P - D -
    I       I       I       I         I       I       I       I
    A       T       C       G         A       G       T       T
```

and

```
    T       A       G       C         T       C       A       A
    I       I       I       I         I       I       I       I
P - D - P - D - P - D - P - D -   P - D - P - D - P - D - P - D -
```

This is often a temporary change, however, because if we allow the DNA to cool down, the strands will usually come back together and form the original double-stranded structure.

The way in which DNA strands separate and rejoin illustrates the types of chemical bonds that hold the different parts of DNA together. The bonds connecting the deoxyriboses to the phosphates and to the bases are strong enough so that they are not easily broken by heating. But the bonds holding pairs of bases together are quite different. They are weak and easily broken by an increase in temperature. When the bonds between the bases are broken, there is nothing to hold the strands together, and they separate.

If the bonds between the bases in DNA are so

weak, what makes them stay together at all? Two bases will stay together only if the chemical shape of one base allows it to fit closely to another base, much like pieces in a jigsaw puzzle. Only two combinations of bases fit this well. One combination is adenine with thymine, and the other is cytosine with guanine. In the following diagram, we have shown these combinations by using different geometric shapes for the bases:

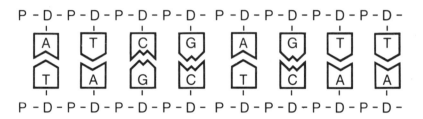

No other combinations of bases fit well enough, and therefore the only pairings normally found in DNA are A-T, T-A, C-G, and G-C.

The bases hold the two strands of DNA together, but they are also important in other ways. You will learn more about this when we examine the genetic code and other information contained in DNA. For now it is enough to say that the information in DNA is in the *sequence* or order of the bases.

Since the information is in the bases and not in the deoxyribose or phosphate, a simpler diagram of DNA can be used. For example, each deoxyribose-phosphate chain can be shown as a line, and the order of the bases can be shown using the four letters for abbreviations of the four bases. Such a diagram of a section of DNA would look like this:

```
A T C G A G T T
T A G C T C A A
```

An even shorter version is to omit the two lines, leaving just the bases, like this:

```
A T C G A G T T
T A G C T C A A
```

These diagrams are quite satisfactory because the deoxyribose-phosphate chain is always the same. Only the sequence of bases varies in different pieces of DNA.

Any sequence of bases is possible in DNA. Some of the many sequences that can exist are

```
A A G G C G
G C A T T T A
G A T G C A T G
C G G G T T A G
T C A A G C G T A
```

An interesting feature of DNA is that if you know the base sequence of one strand, you automatically know the sequence of bases in the opposite strand because of the way that the bases combine. For example, if the first sequence given above—A A G G C G—is in one strand of DNA, the opposite strand would have this sequence—T T C C G C.

Try writing the sequence of bases in the opposite strands for all the sequences shown to make yourself familiar with base pairing. Remember that whenever there is an A, there will be a T in the other strand and that a C will be paired with a G, a G with a C, and a T with an A. Then you might try writing down other possible base sequences for different lengths of DNA and figure out their opposites.

We have seen that all the information in DNA is in the sequence of the bases. It may surprise you that it is possible to have a vast amount of information contained in something as simple as the order or sequence of four bases. But this is not at all unusual. Computers, for example, use as their source of information only two possibilities instead of four—the presence or absence of an electrical impulse. The Morse Code is equally simple, using combinations of dots and dashes to code for letters. The letters can then be combined in many ways to give the information that makes up a language.

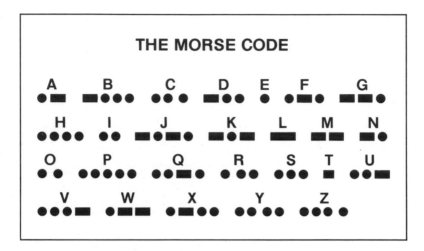

But just what is the information in DNA? This question is not easy to answer because DNA has different kinds of information, some of which we don't completely understand. There is one type of information, however, that we have known about for some time. This information is in the form of a code, the genetic code. The cell uses this code when it performs an important function, making proteins.

2
CELLS, PROTEIN, AND DNA

Cells are the building blocks of all living things. Most plants and animals are made up of many cells, although some consist of only a single cell. The body of a human being has more than 10 trillion cells.

Human cells have different sizes and shapes, depending upon where they are in the body and what role they play. Nerve cells, for example, are extremely long so they can transmit impulses, whereas cells on the surface of linings such as the inner lining of the heart tend to be flat. Many cells are compact and rounded, such as those in glands.

In spite of their variety, cells have many features in common. All cells are semi-liquid in nature and are enclosed by a membrane. Nearly all have an inner region or sphere, the **nucleus**, which is also surrounded by a membrane. DNA is located in this part of the cell, making the nucleus the information center of the cell. All cells have a **cytoplasm**, the part of the cell outside the nucleus. It is in the cytoplasm that the information in DNA is used to form proteins.

Proteins are substances needed for all of the many processes that take place in our bodies, such as growth and the production of energy. Some proteins form the structures of cells. Other proteins, known as **enzymes**, are responsible for nearly everything that goes on inside the cell. This includes such things as burning sugar and fat for energy, breaking down food during digestion, and forming pigment. Enzymes often do their work in special structures located in the cytoplasm. The best known of such structures are the **mitochondria**. The enzymes in mitochondria specialize in energy production.

Like DNA, enzymes and other proteins consist of long chains. Each protein is made up of one or more chains of chemical units called **amino acids** connected to each other. Some proteins have fewer amino acids than others and are therefore smaller in size. Proteins are different not only in size but also in the arrangement of their amino acids. There are 20 amino acids, and they can be arranged in different orders to form many different proteins. Proteins are a lot like the words in a language, which can be short or long and have many combinations of letters.

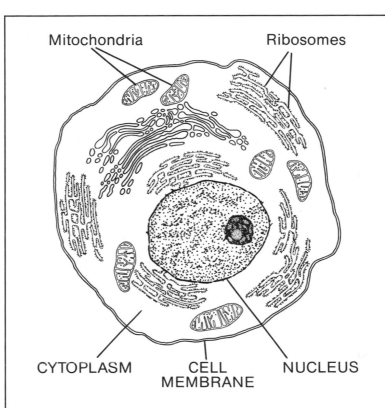

Mitochondria   Ribosomes

CYTOPLASM   CELL   NUCLEUS
             MEMBRANE

This drawing shows some of the parts of a typical human cell. The *nucleus*, the inner region of the cell, contains DNA. Surrounding the nucleus is the *cytoplasm*, where the information in DNA is used to form proteins. Tiny round bodies called *ribosomes* serve as the centers of protein production. Some of the proteins known as enzymes do their work in the *mitochondria*, small structures in the cytoplasm that produce energy.

It is the DNA in a cell's nucleus that controls the "spelling" of the protein language. The coded information in the DNA tells the cell the order of the amino acids in a protein chain and also the length of the chain. In addition to coded information, DNA also includes important signals. For example, there is a signal or special sequence of bases that tells the cell where the information starts in DNA for the order of amino acids in a protein.

The information that DNA contains is found in the cell nucleus (remember that DNA is deoxyribo-*nucleic* acid), but the production of proteins takes place in the cytoplasm. Does the DNA leave the nucleus in order to do its most important job? The nuclear membrane does have holes or pores in it, and chemicals do pass through these holes to and from the cytoplasm. But DNA molecules are very large, too large to get through the openings. DNA always stays in the nucleus.

Packaging DNA   If all the DNA in the nucleus were stretched out, it would extend far beyond the boundaries of the cell. DNA has to be shortened or packaged in some way in order for it to fit inside the nucleus. The need to pack information into a small space is not unique to DNA. A video tape is packaged by being wound around itself and put into a cassette. DNA is also wound, but in a very different way. Inside the nucleus, lengths of DNA are wound around small balls made up of protein. They form structures called **nucleosomes**, which look something like beads on a string when viewed through a powerful microsope.

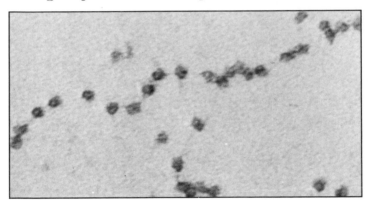

The "strings" of nucleosomes also seem to be wound or twisted in order to shorten DNA even further. Scientists do not completely understand the way in which DNA is packaged inside the nucleus, and they hope to learn more about this important area of research.

3
THE MESSAGE

We have seen that the information in DNA is in the sequence of bases. This information tells the order of amino acids when a protein is formed. But what we have learned about the cell presents us with a puzzle. If DNA stays in the nucleus, how can its information be used for the formation of proteins, which takes place in the cytoplasm? The answer is that the information is carried from the nucleus to the cytoplasm by means of a different version of DNA, known as **RNA**. Since it carries the genetic information as a kind of message, we call it **messenger RNA** or mRNA for short.

Messenger RNA is formed in the nucleus using a portion of DNA as a model. The RNA has only one strand and is shorter than DNA. Therefore it can pass through the pores in the nuclear membrane to get from the nucleus to the cytoplasm. There the information in RNA is used to form proteins. Usually a cell needs many copies of a protein, and several copies of RNA are formed from a section of DNA. Later, you will learn about other types of RNA besides mRNA that are also needed to make proteins. They too are formed in the nucleus and pass from there into the cytoplasm.

We now need to find out what RNA is in order to understand how it can be formed with DNA as a model and how it can have the same information that is in DNA. RNA stands for the words *ribonucleic acid*. It is a chemical substance similar to DNA, except that it has a different sugar and one of the bases is different. Instead of deoxyribose, RNA has the sugar known as **ribose (R)**, and instead of thymine, it has a slightly different base called **uracil (U)**. The other three bases are the same as in DNA. A segment of RNA would look like this:

```
P - R - P - R - P - R - P - R -  P - R - P - R - P - R - P - R -
    |       |       |       |        |       |       |       |
    U       A       C       C        G       U       G       A
```

As with DNA, the information is in the sequence of the bases. Therefore, we can shorten this diagram and show the sugars and phosphates as a line, just as we did for DNA, but here we will use a dashed line, - - - - - -, instead of a solid line. The RNA would then look like this:

$$\overline{\text{U A C C G U G A}}$$

Or we can just show the bases. Even if we simplify the diagram in this way, we can still tell that it is RNA and not DNA, since uracil is present and thymine is absent.

RNA carries the same information as DNA because it has the same base sequence, and it has the same base sequence because of the way it is formed. Let's look at an example to see how this happens. Here is a section of DNA that will be used in forming the RNA. (Remember that real DNA would be much longer and in the shape of a spiral.)

```
T  A  T  C  G  A  T  A  C  C  G  T  G  A  G  C  T  A  G
A  T  A  G  C  T  A  T  G  G  C  A  C  T  C  G  A  T  C
```

Before RNA is formed, the strands in a section of DNA unwind and open up in this manner:

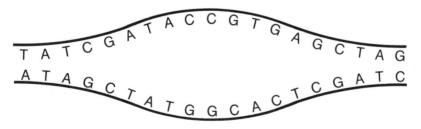

Then bases, sugars, and phosphates that are present in the nucleus join with part of the DNA to form RNA. In this diagram, RNA is shown in **bold letters**:

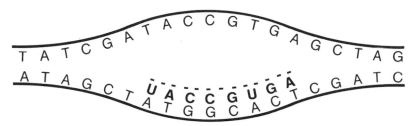

Take a good look at the example and you will notice several things. For instance, only one strand of RNA is formed. Also, the bases in RNA are paired with the bases in only one of the DNA strands. Notice that the pairing is the same as between the bases in DNA, except that the base in RNA that pairs with adenine is not thymine, since RNA has none. Instead uracil in RNA pairs with adenine. Notice also that the sequence of bases in RNA is the same as in the opposite section of the other DNA strand (the one on top) except that uracil is present in RNA where thymine is found in DNA.

The reason for the similar base sequence in RNA is that, when RNA is formed, the bases added are only those that will pair with bases in one of the DNA strands. Like base pairing between two strands of DNA, the RNA bases fit with the DNA bases because they have the proper chemical shape.

After RNA has been formed, it becomes separated from DNA. The RNA then goes from the nucleus to the cytoplasm, carrying the information in its base sequence. After enough copies of RNA have been formed, the two stands of DNA come back together.

When RNA is formed using DNA as a model, we say that the DNA has been transcribed and call the process **transcription.** Transcription is something like your going to the library and copying into a notebook information that is important to you, for example, the directions for making a kite. Perhaps you have done this because the directions are in a reference book that cannot be taken from the library, just as DNA must remain in the nucleus. You have transcribed the directions to take home, where you will use them to make your kite. The directions copied by RNA from DNA are transferred to the cytoplasm, where they will be used to make a protein.

4
THE CODE

As we know, DNA has information coded in the sequence of its bases. This **genetic code** tells the order of amino acids that make up a protein. Because mRNA is transcribed from DNA, it carries the same coded information. Let's take a closer look at this remarkable code.

The genetic code consists of the bases of RNA grouped in series of three's. The groups of three bases are called **codons,** and each codes for a particular amino acid. For example, the codon ACG codes for the amino acid called threonine, and the codon GUC codes for another amino acid, valine.

In a section of mRNA, the first three bases are the first codon, the next three are the second one, and so on. For example, if mRNA has this sequence,

G C A A C G C C G G A A C G C

it will code for a chain of five amino acids. The code tells that the first amino acid will be alanine, because the first codon is GCA, which codes for this amino acid. The second codon is the next three bases, or ACG. This codon codes for amino acid threonine, so this will be the next one in the chain. The third, fourth, and fifth amino acids will be proline, glutamic acid, and arginine, since the next three codons are CCG, GAA, and CGC. The protein chain coded for will therefore have the following sequence of amino acids:

alanine - threonine - proline - glutamic acid - arginine

Chains of amino acids are typically much longer, but our illustration with a short chain is sufficient to show how the code works.

The example of mRNA that we have just given is not complete. The sequence of bases in the mRNA would be more realistic with the addition of two other codons, one on each end:

A U G G C A A C G C C G G A A C G C **U A A**

The added codons are there for a special purpose. The one on the left, AUG, codes for the start of the amino acid chain, whereas the one on the right, UAA, codes for the end of the chain. Two other codons,

UAG and UGA, also code for the end of the chain when present in mRNA. The codon AUG has two roles in the genetic code. When it does not appear at the beginning of a section of mRNA, it codes for the amino acid methionine rather than for the start of the chain of amino acids. But UAA, UAG, and UGA never code for an amino acid. They code only for the end of the chain.

When the information in mRNA is used to form a chain of amino acids, we say that the coded message has been read. The proper amino acids are connected to each other, and we then have a protein or the beginning of one. Like words in a language, the code is read in only one direction, starting at AUG and ending at UAA, UAG, or UGA. The direction of reading or the flow of information is sometimes described as occurring from "upstream" to "downstream," like the direction of the flow of water in a river.

The message is never read in the reverse direction and would be quite different if it was. For example, GCA codes for the amino acid called alanine. If read in the reverse direction, the codon would be ACG and would code for an entirely different amino acid, threonine. In the same way, the word "was" becomes an entirely different word, "saw," when read or spelled backwards.

The message in a section of mRNA is something like a sentence with a beginning and an end but no punctuation in between. There is no extra space or stop marks between the codons. The cell automatically takes the first three bases after AUG to code for the first amino acid, the next three to code for the next one, and so on. This means that the message in RNA would be different if, for some reason, a pair of bases was missing from the original DNA. There would then be a base missing in the mRNA formed from the DNA. Because the code is read automatically, it would be read "out of frame" for each amino acid coded for after the missing base.

You can illustrate this for yourself by figuring out the order of amino acids if the first cytosine, C, is missing from the base sequence given earlier for mRNA.

A U G G Ⓒ A A C G C C G G A A C G C **U A A**

You will find that the amino acids are completely different. For example, the first amino acid will be glutamic acid instead of alanine. With this kind of change in the bases, the protein formed from the amino acid chain would also be changed.

The genetic code has been known since the late 1950s and early 1960s. The story of deciphering the code is a lasting monument to the persistence and ingenuity of scientists. "Cracking" the code would have been simple if the amino acid sequence in a protein could have been matched with the sequence of bases in RNA. But at the time the code was deciphered, it was not possible to determine the base sequence of long pieces of RNA or DNA. Scientists had to devise special experiments to get around the problem. When they did, they found that the genetic code seemed to be the same for all forms of life, from the simplest to the most complex. Recently, however, a few exceptions to this rule have been reported. For example, in two species of the single-celled animals known as protozoa, UAA codes for glutamine instead of for the end of a protein. Other exceptions may be found in the future as the cells of more species are studied.

THE GENETIC CODE

CODON	*AMINO ACID*
AAA, AAG	lysine
AAC, AAU	asparagine
ACA, ACC, ACG, ACU	threonine
AGA, AGG	arginine
AGC, AGU	serine
AUA, AUC, AUU	isoleucine
AUG	methionine
AUG	start of protein
CAA, CAG	glutamine
CAC, CAU	histidine
CCA, CCC, CCG, CCU	proline
CGA, CGC, CGG, CGU	arginine
CUA, CUC, CUG, CUU	leucine
GAA, GAG	glutamic acid
GAC, GAU	aspartic acid
GCA, GCC, GCG, GGU	alanine
GGA, GGC, GGG, GGU	glycine
GUA, GUC, GUG, GUU	valine
UAA, UAG	end of protein
UAC, UAU	tyrosine
UCA, UCC, UCG, UCU	serine
UGA	end of protein
UGC, UGU	cysteine
UGG	tryptophan
UUA, UUG	leucine
UUC, UUU	phenylalanine

5

TRANSLATING THE MESSAGE

The reading of the message in mRNA in order to form a protein is accomplished by a very complex process. We call this process **translation**, and when it has been completed, we say that the message has been translated. We use these words because the reading process resembles translating one language into another, for example, Spanish into English. In this case, however, the cell is translating base sequence into amino acid sequence to form protein.

Translation takes place in the cytoplasm of the cell by means of a unique assembly-line system. In the cytoplasm, there are many small, figure-eight-shaped structures called **ribosomes**. They look something like this:

There are also many copies of the different amino acids, as yet unconnected to each other. To start the assembly line, the mRNA is threaded through a ribosome.

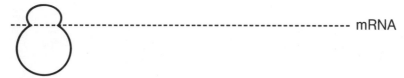

Then the ribosome moves down the mRNA. In doing so, it reads the coded message and connects amino acids brought from the cytoplasm. In the early stages, the process looks like this:

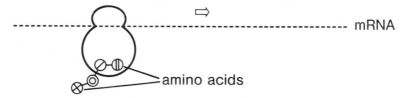

and later like this,

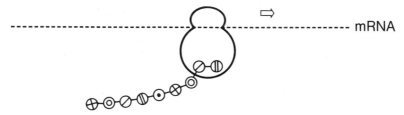

Still later, the ribosome is near the end of the mRNA, and almost all of the amino acids are connected.

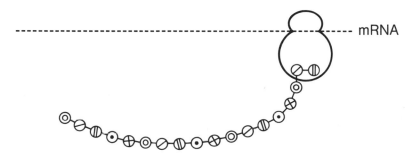

When the ribosome has finished reading the message, the chain of amino acids becomes separated from the ribosome, as does the mRNA. The ribosomes and mRNA are used again—many times—to connect more amino acids to form more proteins.

We have just described the assembly of a protein but have not given the details of this very complicated process. One of the details has to do with transportation. When anything is assembled, there must be some way to bring the parts together in one place. Many times our hands do this, for instance, when we are assembling a model car from a kit. We pick up each piece and put it with the other pieces we are joining together. Something similar takes place, but on a larger scale, in the assembly line of an automobile factory, although here the "hands" may be those of a robot.

The same need for transportation exists in the assembly of a protein. There must be some way to bring the correct amino acids to the ribosome so that they can be connected to each other. This job is done by another form of RNA, **transfer RNA (tRNA)**. Like mRNA, tRNA is formed in the nucleus from a portion of DNA and then passes through the pores in the nuclear membrane into the cytoplasm. A section of transfer RNA is quite short and folded on itself, somewhat like the wire in a coat hanger. At any one time, there are many tRNAs in the cytoplasm, ready to play their role in protein production.

Let's take a look at a diagram showing tRNA in action. (The actual shape of tRNA is simplified here.)

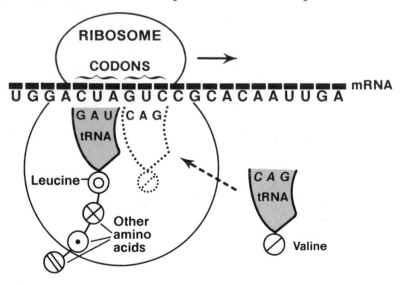

In this diagram, leucine has just been added to the chain of amino acids, shown on the left. The ribosome is now reading the next codon in the mRNA, the one on the right side. This codon, GUC, codes for valine. The tRNA on the right is in the process of bringing valine to the ribosome.

Why does valine arrive at the ribosome at exactly the time it is needed to add to the protein? The amino acid is delivered at just the right moment because it is attached to a section of tRNA that "matches" the valine codon being read by the ribosome at that moment. The tRNA has three bases, CAG, at the end opposite to where the valine is attached. These bases are called the **anticodon** because each of them has the proper shape to pair with one of the bases of the valine codon, GUC, just like a piece in a jigsaw puzzle. The other amino acids in the cytoplasm are attached to different tRNAs whose anticodons will not pair with the GUC codon.

When the tRNA carrying the valine arrives at the ribosome, the bases in its anticodon pair with the bases in the mRNA. This pairing keeps the tRNA in the ribosome long enough for the valine to be connected to leucine in the amino acid chain. What happens next is shown in another diagram.

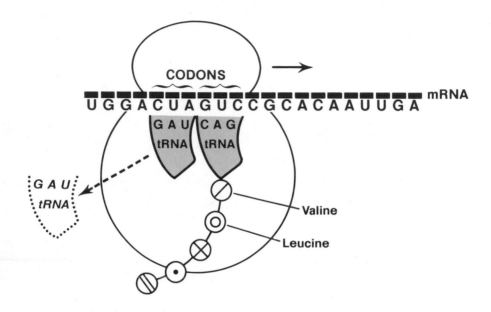

Valine is now connected to leucine, but in such a way that the chain of amino acids is attached to the tRNA in the right side of the ribosome instead of the one in the left side. The tRNA on the left has served its purpose and now leaves the ribosome. After picking up another leucine in the cytoplasm, it will be ready for use again whenever leucine is needed in an amino acid chain.

In the next step of the assembly-line process, the ribosome moves down one codon. This stage can be seen in the following diagram.

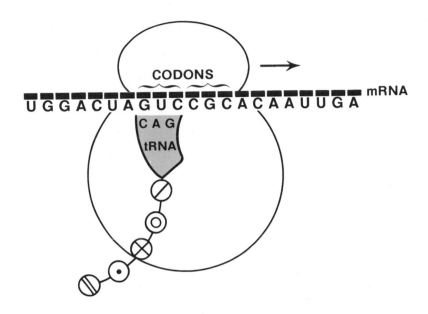

At this point a cycle has been completed, and an amino acid added to the chain. Notice how similar this diagram is to the first one. The main difference is that there is one more amino acid in the chain and the ribosome has moved down one codon.

A new cycle is started when the codon on the right attracts a different tRNA with a different amino acid. With each cycle, an amino acid is added as the ribosome moves down mRNA three bases at a time. This continues as long as codons are present that code for an amino acid.

The assembly of a protein within the cell cytoplasm is as automated as the assembly of a car on a modern production line. If an important part is not available, then production comes to a halt.

Reading the coded message in mRNA by this assembly-line process is precise, but highly automated. If, for some reason, any of the different amino acids or tRNAs are missing from the cytoplasm, the whole process will stop whenever that amino acid or tRNA is needed. It will also stop if the next codon to be read does not code for an amino acid. One such codon is UAA, which codes instead for the end of a protein. There is no tRNA with an anticodon whose bases will pair with UAA. The absence of an appropriate tRNA means that translation cannot continue once UAA is reached, no matter how many bases there might be after this codon. Because of this, UAA is able to code for the end of the amino acid chain and stop protein formation.

In looking back over the process of protein formation, it may seem to you that the ribosome does not have a very important part to play. After all, it is mRNA that contains the coded message and tRNA that brings the amino acids together. But the amino acids cannot actually be connected without the ribosome to hold tRNAs in place. The ribosome is able to do this because it has two spaces that are each the right size and shape to be occupied by tRNA, much like a key fitting into a lock. These spaces hold the two tRNAs next to each other in the ribosome so that their amino acids can be connected.

Another type of RNA, **ribosomal RNA (rRNA)**, may also assist in the proper positioning of the tRNAs in the ribosome. Some of the bases in rRNA may pair with some of the tRNA bases that are not part of the anticodon. This would help to hold the two tRNAs next to each other in the ribosome. Scientists are not sure about the exact role of rRNA in protein production, but they do know that rRNAs are found in the ribosome. There are also many proteins in the ribosome, which is a very complex structure still being studied.

What have we learned so far about DNA and its role in the cell? We have described the nature of DNA and the way in which the information it contains is put to use. We have seen that mRNA is formed in the nucleus when bases, phosphates, and sugars are connected together. This takes place in such a way that the sequence of bases in the coded message is copied from a section of DNA. In the cytoplasm, mRNA is threaded through a ribosome. The message is then read or translated by joining amino acids that are brought to the ribosome by tRNAs.

In the next two chapters, we will learn about some of our newer knowledge of DNA, including the changes that must be made in RNA before translation can take place and the signals in DNA and RNA that are essential in order to use the coded information.

6

PROCESSING THE INFORMATION

We have known the genetic code for some time and understood how the message in mRNA is translated. We have recently discovered, however, that using the information contained in DNA to make proteins is much more complicated than was originally thought. Most of our newer knowledge has come from improved procedures for studying DNA and RNA. We have found that after RNA is formed in the nucleus, it is changed or processed in several ways before passing into the cytoplasm. We have also discovered that messenger RNA is more than just a series of codons.

The part of mRNA that we have already described is the central part, known as the **coding region.** This section contains codons, starting with AUG and ending with one of the codons for the end of a protein, such as UAA. There are, however, other parts of the mRNA, both in front of AUG and after UAA. These parts, known as **leader** and **trailer sections**, are shown in the following diagram.

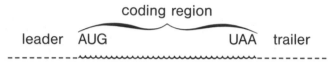

The leader and trailer sections have no codons and therefore contain no coded information for amino acid sequence. Instead, they play other roles in translation. So far we don't know much about the trailer section, but we are starting to understand the function of the leader section.

The leader attaches the mRNA to the ribosome in such a way that translation will begin at the proper spot, namely the first codon, AUG. To understand how the leader works, it is helpful to think of other kinds of information that have a special "starting" section. For example, a movie cannot be shown until the projectionist threads the first part of the film through the projector to get it started and in frame. This first portion of the film has no pictures on it but serves only to insert the film into the projector. Cassette tapes also have a small section that produces no sound but is there for attachment of the tape.

In addition to the function of the leader and trailer

sections, scientists are learning about the processing of mRNA before it leaves the nucleus. These changes in mRNA take place primarily in higher forms of life such as green plants and animals, including humans. Since they have been discovered only recently, scientists are just beginning to understand their significance.

The RNA formed in the nucleus is usually longer than the mRNA that goes from the nucleus to the cytoplasm. One of the changes in processing is simply the cutting off of one end, like this,

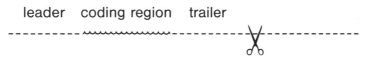

leader   coding region   trailer

Besides shortening of RNA, there are two changes that involve additions:

leader   coding region   trailer   poly-A tail

CAP----------~~~~~~~~~~~----------wwwwwwwwwwwww

Notice that one addition, a **cap**, is at the upstream end, and the other, a **poly-A tail**, is at the downstream end. The cap has a single base in it, a guanine that has been modified. Like the leader section of mRNA, the cap is important for the proper attachment of mRNA to the ribosome so that translation can start.

The addition at the opposite end, the poly-A tail, is a long series of 100 or more bases that are all adenine. (Poly-A means "Many As.") The poly-A tail is not found in all mRNAs of the same cell and is not necessary for the code to be translated. Scientists are not sure about its function but think that this addition probably helps to protect the mRNA from breakdown or destruction so it will last longer.

The three changes we have described take place at the ends of the RNA. There is still one more change, not shown so far in our diagrams. This involves removal of sections from the middle of RNA. When RNA is originally formed, the coding region is actually not continuous but interrupted, as shown here:

AUG   UAA

The parts with dashed lines represent sections of RNA that do not have codons. We call them **intervening sequences**. They are removed during processing so that the coding region is continuous and without interruption. Therefore, the mRNA entering the cytoplasm lacks the intervening sequences, and its coding region is like this:

AUG   UAA

The discovery of interruptions within the coding region of RNA was completely unexpected, and it is still difficult to understand this arrangement of the information. Most of the simpler forms of life such as bacteria do not have interruptions. They are typically found in the more complex forms. Our diagram showed two interruptions, but sometimes there are more. Regardless of how many there are, they are all removed during processing. Then the coding parts are connected or spliced to each other.

Since RNA is formed by transcribing DNA, the noncoding gaps are also found in DNA. Their presence within the coded message has caused us to change our idea of the nature of portions of DNA that are called **genes**. We consider a gene to be a part of DNA that has within it the coded message for the amino acid sequence of a single protein, plus adjacent parts like the leader that are necessary to use the message. Like recordings of several songs on a single tape, there are many genes on one long piece of DNA. We can't see where a gene is, just as we can't see where the different songs are on a tape.

When RNA is transcribed from DNA, it contains the coded message for the amino acid sequence of a single protein. But, as we have seen, RNA often has intervening sequences in its coding region. These same interruptions must also exist in DNA, where they separate parts of the coding region of genes. This fact has caused scientists to realize that there are

split genes—a completely new idea.

A good way to understand why the discovery of such genes was so unexpected is to imagine what this would be like if it were found in another type of information, such as the recording of a song on tape. Think how surprised you would be if you bought a tape in which each song was interrupted several times by sections of silence or noise and that the only way you could play the song without interruption would be to splice out the unwanted sections. It would be hard to imagine why such a tape would be produced in the first place, and the same is true for split genes. It seems wasteful and unnecessary for the cell to form a long piece of RNA and then to remove sections. Furthermore, not all genes in the same cell have interruptions.

But genes with interruptions do exist and are transcribed. It is absolutely essential for the interruptions to be removed from the RNA formed by the transcription and the parts of each coding region spliced together. Since the code is read automatically, the interruptions will be taken as part of the message in mRNA if they are not removed. As a result, the wrong protein will be formed. This can be life-threatening, since proteins are vital for the functioning of the body.

We are starting to learn how intervening sequences

are removed and how the parts of the coding region are spliced together. An intervening sequence between two parts of the coding region,

is cut at one end and forms a loop or lariat.

Then the intervening sequence is snipped off. The coding parts are joined so that they are continuous with each other.

A special type of RNA, called **snRNA (small nuclear RNA)**, is needed for the removal of intervening sequences. This RNA, like the others, is formed in the nucleus by transcription of DNA. But unlike them, it does not pass into the cytoplasm.

HOW RNA IS PROCESSED

RNA FORMED IN THE NUCLEUS

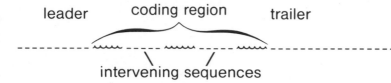

leader　　　coding region　　　trailer

intervening sequences

mRNA TRANSFERRED FROM THE NUCLEUS TO THE CYTOPLASM

leader　coding region　trailer　poly-A tail

CAP

The RNA formed in the nucleus by transcription is longer than the mRNA that passes into the cytoplasm. While in the nucleus, RNA is modified in four different ways: (1) Intervening sequences within the coding region are removed; (2) A section at the downstream end is cut off; (3) A cap is added at the upstream end; (4) A poly-A tail is added at the downstream end.

7
SIGNALS

Some of the new research in genetics has helped us to achieve a better understanding of the noncoding regions in DNA and RNA. As we saw in the last chapter, parts of DNA like the leader and the intervening sequences do not have codons. Even though they lack codons, these regions do have certain sequences of bases that are vital for use of the coded message in RNA and DNA. It is only in recent years that new research techniques have made it possible for us to find out what these sequences are and what role they play. This new information is the subject of this chapter—base sequences that serve as signals.

There are several kinds of signals in the noncoding regions of DNA and RNA. Some tell, for example, where transcription of DNA will start and end and where the intervening sequences are in RNA. Such signals are important because they insure accuracy of transcription, processing, and translation. These are the steps that take place when the information in DNA is used. A mistake in any of these steps usually results in loss of the coded information. For example, if transcription of RNA starts in the center of a coding region instead of the beginning, only part of the RNA will be formed. The resulting chain of amino acids will then be too short.

The presence of signals in DNA and RNA is not unexpected. Life is full of signals that tell us where something begins and ends, or when to do something. Signals may be such things as signs along the road telling where construction starts and ends or when to slow down because you have reached a congested area. Or the signals may be more complicated, like those that tell where different pieces of data are stored on a computer tape or disk. Our written language has signals, too. Thus a period signals the end of one sentence, and a capital letter the start of the next one. All these signals are important in their own way, and so are the ones in DNA and RNA. Let's take a look at some of them.

The signal for the beginning of transcription in DNA is particularly important, and we have known about it the longest. Each gene in DNA has been found to have within its beginning section a sequence of bases that tells where transcription of RNA will begin. The sequences may be slightly different in different genes, but these are always present: T A T A

A T A T

We usually reduce this to T A T A, the sequence in one of the strands.

It makes sense that the signal for the start of transcription contains the bases adenine and thymine and lacks cytosine and guanine. Adenine and thymine have only two chemical bonds to hold them next to each other when in adjacent strands of DNA, but guanine and cytosine have three. Since transcription starts with the opening up and separation of the two strands of DNA, it would be easier to start the separation in a section containing adenine and thymine, since they are held together by fewer bonds than cytosine and guanine.

We know what the signal is, but how is it recognized as the place for transcription to begin? It is recognized by the **enzyme of transcription.** An enzyme is a type of protein that has the ability to cause a chemical change to take place. The enzyme of transcription causes RNA to be formed by connecting bases, sugars, and phosphates. This enzyme recognizes the T A T A sequence wherever it occurs in DNA and starts transcription near this spot.

Transcription is not continuous; it stops as well as

starts at a certain point in DNA. So there must also be a series of bases that is a signal for stopping transcription. Part of the stopping signal is known. It consists of a series of thymines, one after another.

As we have learned, RNA is processed after it is formed in higher forms of life. One of the changes of processing is the removal of a section at the downstream end. Although we don't know why the section removed is there in the first place, we do know that the RNA is cut at one certain spot and that the poly-A tail is then added. So it is not surprising that there is a signal in RNA for where the cut will be made. Part of the signal is always A A U A A A. If, for some reason, any of these bases are different, the RNA will be cut less efficiently or not at all.

Another important set of signals tells where each intervening sequence begins and ends. This is vital because, if even one additional base or one base less is removed during processing, the code will be read out of frame, and much of the message will be lost. We can illustrate this best by an example. Suppose the coding region has the following base sequence:

A U G G C A A C G C C G G A A C G C U A A

Suppose also that there is an intervening sequence

within the coding region that must be removed during processing before the message can be translated. In the following illustration, small letters are used for the bases in the intervening sequence. (Intervening sequences are typically longer, but a smaller number of bases is less awkward to use.)

A U G G C A A g u c a c g g c u u c g c u a g C G C C G G A A C G C U A A

Notice that the intervening sequence starts with *gu* and ends with *ag*. This is true for all intervening sequences studied so far. Scientists believe that these two pairs of bases are part of the signals for the beginning and end of intervening sequences.

The example can also be used to show what would happen if these signals are not recognized properly. Suppose that all of the bases of the intervening sequence were removed in processing except for the first one, *g*, which was retained. The base sequence would then be:

A U G G C A A g C G C C G G A A C G C U A A

With the inclusion of the *g*, the amino acids coded for after the intervening sequence will be different. You can see this for yourself by figuring out the amino acid sequence using the genetic code, given in

Chapter 4. Then compare this to the amino acids coded for if all bases of the intervening sequence had been removed. This shows what can happen with just a slight error during processing. Removal of intervening sequences and splicing must be done with great accuracy, or RNA will lose much of its information during processing.

There are other signals in RNA as well. One of these is in the leader section of mRNA. The sequence A G G A has been found in this portion of the mRNA in bacteria. These bases are part of a signal telling where translation of the amino acid sequence will start. They attach the mRNA to the ribosome in such a way that translation will start at the first AUG codon.

We have now reached the point where we have discussed the different types of information in DNA and how the information is used. We have yet to describe how the information is copied and how it can be changed. These are the subjects of the remaining chapters in this book.

SOME SIGNALS IN DNA AND RNA

BASE SEQUENCE   TYPE OF SIGNAL

In DNA

T A T A . . . . For starting transcription

Several thymines . . For stopping transcription

In RNA

A A U A A A . . . . For cutting the downstream end in processing

G U . . . . Where an intervening sequence begins

A G . . . . Where an intervening sequence ends

A G G A . . . . For attachment of mRNA to the ribosome

8

COPYING THE INFORMATION

It is often necessary to make copies of different kinds of information. When you are writing on a word processor, you usually make a back-up copy of your floppy disk to be sure that the information is not accidentally lost. Sometimes it is necessary to make multiple copies of an important document on a photocopy machine so that everyone in a group can have a copy. Millions of copies, each exactly alike, are made of the information in magazines, books, records, and tapes.

There are times when it is necessary to have exact copies of the DNA in a cell. When a cell divides in the normal growth process, each new cell must receive a copy of the vital information contained in the DNA. The cell is able to make copies of its DNA, and this is one of its most important functions.

The process by which DNA is copied is called **replication.** Replication is like transcription in some ways. The two strands of DNA separate, and new bases, along with sugars and phosphates, are joined to the existing bases. A simple diagram shows this, using **bold** for new DNA.

Original DNA	Separated Strands	Duplicated DNA
	T C G G A A	T C G G A A **A G C C T T**
T C G G A A A G C C T T $\Rightarrow$	$\Rightarrow$	
	A G C C T T	**T C G G A A** A G C C T T

Notice that, unlike transcription, replication produces *two* new DNA strands. The result is duplicate copies of the section of DNA, each copy with the same base sequence. The base sequences are the same because during replication the only new bases added are those that will pair with bases in the original strands of DNA. For example, when the strands separate,

T C G G A A

A G C C T T

the new bases added to the first two existing bases are

T C G G A A
A

and

T
A G C C T T

since adenine pairs with thymine and thymine pairs
with adenine. No other bases will be added at this
spot because only these two will fit, like pieces added
to a jigsaw puzzle. In the same way, the other bases
will be paired with their complementary bases. After
replication, therefore, the base sequence is the same
in each copy of DNA.

Replication takes place just before a cell is ready
to divide. After division, there are two cells instead
of one, and each contains DNA identical to that of
the original cell. During its lifetime, a cell may divide
thousands of times. Each time, replication produces
an accurate copy of the cell's DNA so that the new
cells can use its information in making proteins and
performing their other tasks.

REPLICATION COMPARED TO TRANSCRIPTION

ORIGINAL DNA

Strands open up

REPLICATION	*TRANSCRIPTION*
DNA formed	RNA formed

End result	**End result**
DNA	DNA
and	and
DNA	RNA

RNA and new DNA are shown in bold.

Scientists have gained a better understanding of genetics by using new methods of studying DNA. Here a researcher is seen examining pieces of DNA shown in a photographic negative produced by a technique known as gel electrophoresis.

9

CHANGING THE
INFORMATION

Most information can be changed in one way or another. When you reuse a VCR tape by taping something new onto it, for example, you are permanently changing the information on the tape. Sometimes this happens by mistake when you accidentally reuse a tape that you wanted to keep. The information on a computer's floppy disk can also be changed either by deliberately adding and erasing material or by an accidental erasure.

The information in DNA can also be changed in several different ways. Usually these changes are the result of accidents that occur during the life of a cell. Recent developments in genetics have also made it possible to bring about deliberate changes in DNA by using the methods of recombinant DNA. This chapter will look at both of these ways in which DNA is changed.

Some of the most common changes in DNA occur during replication. They are caused by mistakes such as the addition of the wrong base to one of the strands. For example, when replication takes place, thymine might be paired with guanine instead of adenine to give:

T C G G A A
<u>G</u>

If all the rest of the bases added are the correct ones, the new DNA will look like this:

T C G G A A
Ⓖ G C C T T

Fortunately, the enzyme responsible for replication has some of the capabilities of a word processing program. It can proofread the base pairing and correct any mistake that it detects. This eliminates most of the wrong pairings that might be made during replication. The proofreading is not perfect, however, and sometimes the mistake goes undetected. Then we get a permanent change in the information in DNA, which we call a **mutation**.

It takes a second replication of the DNA to get the mutation in both strands, like this:

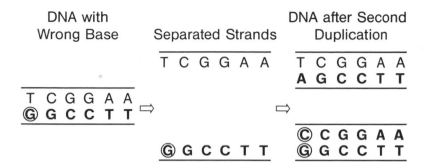

When the DNA with the wrong base replicates a second time, the bases in each strand are joined by the appropriate bases—T with A and G with C. Since the G was a mistake, however, this second replication produces a completely incorrect base pair—

$$\overline{\underline{\begin{matrix} C \\ G \end{matrix}}} \quad - \qquad \text{instead of} \qquad \overline{\underline{\begin{matrix} T \\ A \end{matrix}}} \quad -$$

the original pair before the first replication took place.

Mutations change the base sequence and therefore the information in DNA. If they are in the coding region, the message in mRNA will be changed as well as the protein that it codes for. What effect this has depends on which protein is changed and in what way. Some mutations have minor effects. Others have serious consequences, like the change responsible for sickle-cell anemia. In this mutation, blood cells are misshapen and fewer in number because of the substitution of a single amino acid—valine for glutamic acid—in the protein hemoglobin.

If a mutation changes a protein that is an enzyme, it may then be impossible for the enzyme to function. This is the case with the condition known as albinism. Individuals with this condition lack color in their skin, hair, and eyes because of a change in one of the enzymes needed for pigment formation.

Both albinism and sickle-cell anemia are caused by mutations that can be inherited. The changes are present in the DNA of reproductive cells and are passed on from parents to children. Mutations that take place in the DNA of body cells like those in the liver or bone marrow affect only the person in whom the change has occurred.

There are many other examples of mutations that can be passed on from one generation to another. Such mutations, occurring over millions of years, probably account for most of the physical differences among humans. Some of the differences caused by mutations are small and unimportant, for instance, variations in the way people's ear lobes are attached. Other differences are of greater significance, however, and affect a wide range of characteristics, such as height, sensitivity to sunlight, the ability of blood to clot, and color vision. Mutations also account for the existence of many of the differences found in other forms of life, for example, albino robins, white tigers, double-pawed cats, and yellow roses.

The mutations we have just described are caused by a replacement of bases by other bases. This, however, is not the only way that DNA can be changed. Another type of mutation occurs when the bases are rearranged. This can happen when DNA is broken into smaller pieces, for example, when it is exposed to X-rays. The broken pieces sometimes rejoin, but they may be arranged differently. This means that some of the bases will be in a different place in the DNA, although they will not be changed otherwise.

One example of mutation caused by rearrangement was discovered in experiments with a miniature fly called drosophila. Some of the flies were observed to have white patches in their eyes due to an absence of pigment. What had happened was that a gene for eye pigment had been moved to a different spot along the flies' DNA. The gene was still present, but because it was in the wrong place, it was not always transcribed into RNA. We now know that there are several different types of rearrangement of bases. They are apparently more common than once thought, although not as common as mutations involving replacement of bases.

Mutations usually result from accidental changes in DNA. In recent years, however, humans have learned how to make deliberate changes in genetic material. Scientists have discovered a method of rearranging bases in such a way as to produce combinations not found in nature. We call such rearrangements **recombinant DNA.** The techniques used usually involve splicing DNA from one form of life into DNA of another form. For example, a piece of human DNA, shown in **bold,** might be spliced into bacterial DNA, like this:

```
GAATTGACCTAGGCTCTAGGAATTC
CTTAACTGGATCCGAGATCCTTAAG
```

Changing DNA in this manner is known as **genetic engineering.** What makes it possible is that DNA is the same in almost all forms of life. DNA from different organisms can therefore be cut and spliced together, something like combining parts of two movies to form a single film.

Recombinant DNA can be put to use in a wide variety of ways. One example is the production of a human protein, such as insulin, by splicing the gene directing the formation of the protein into DNA of bacteria. The bacteria can be grown in large quantities to produce insulin, which is then extracted and

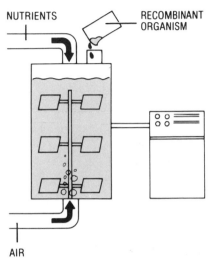

NUTRIENTS

RECOMBINANT
ORGANISM

AIR

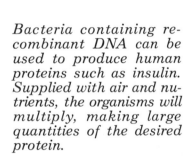

Bacteria containing recombinant DNA can be used to produce human proteins such as insulin. Supplied with air and nutrients, the organisms will multiply, making large quantities of the desired protein.

given to people with diabetes. Some diabetics in the United States are now using insulin produced by recombinant DNA.

Another possible use of recombinant DNA is in the treatment of certain human diseases caused by defective genes. The harmful effects of these diseases — for instance, the uncontrolled bleeding caused by hemophilia—might be prevented by splicing the DNA from a normal person into the DNA of a person with the defective gene. This technique is being studied now, and scientists hope that it will be possible to use it in the future. Recombinant DNA could also be

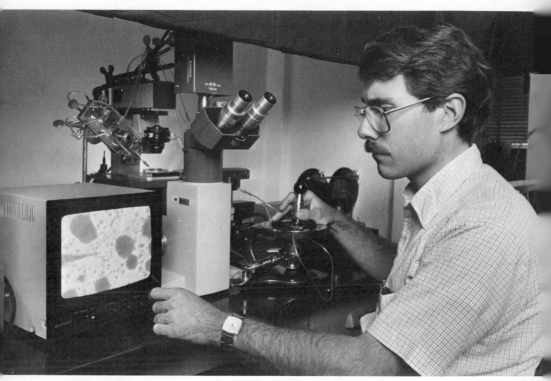

This plant scientist is using a fine glass needle (seen on monitor) to insert genes for salt tolerance into the cell of a petunia plant. New plants produced from the altered cell may be able to grow in salty soil.

used in agriculture to insert genes from one plant into another to get a desired characteristic, such as disease resistance.

The technique for making recombinant DNA is new, and scientists are using it with caution. They want to be sure that they do not produce an undesirable combination of DNA. When human beings take the responsibility of changing DNA into their own hands, they must be careful about the results.

This brings us to the end of our discussion of DNA. You now have a basic understanding of the nature of biological information. This includes knowledge of what DNA is, how it is processed, and how it can be changed. But, most important, you have learned what kind of information DNA contains, how it is expressed in a code and signals, and how it is used to make proteins.

For most of you, this is only a beginning. In one way or another, you will hear more about the subject of DNA in years to come. Our knowledge is increasing at a rapid rate, and it will be interesting to watch for announcements on television and in the newspaper of the new discoveries that await us. Knowing more about DNA will be especially important in future years, as you and others are faced with making decisions on how to apply our new-found knowledge and technology in medicine, agriculture, and industry.

MODELS OF DNA

Making models is a great help in understanding DNA. Models can be made from a wide variety of materials, ranging from inexpensive paper of different colors to carved pieces of wood. We owe much to the use of models, since they were important to scientists in figuring out the make-up of DNA. Even if you are not a scientist, you can make models, either by yourself or as a class or family project.

An example of a simple model of DNA is one made of pieces of colored paper pasted to a sheet of white paper. You can cut out pieces of different colors and shapes to represent the three parts of DNA. You might use red paper for deoxyribose, blue paper for phosphate, and yellow paper for the bases. Then arrange them in the proper manner for a model of double-stranded DNA.

Your model can be made more detailed if you show each of the four bases as a different color and shape. If you do additional reading and learn more about the chemistry of DNA, you can picture the exact shape of each part of DNA, even to the point of showing the individual hydrogens, oxygens, carbons, and nitrogens of which the different parts are composed. A drawing like the one below showing the chemical units in the four bases could be used to create such a model.

Use your imagination and what is on hand when you make models. For example, you could use Ping-Pong balls and yarn to show how DNA is packaged into nucleosomes. Let the yarn represent DNA and the Ping Pong balls the rest of the nucleosome. Wrap the yarn for about two turns around each ball, and hold it there with a washable glue or paste. If, later on, you are no longer interested in the model, the yarn can be removed and the Ping-Pong balls used for their original purpose.

The beauty of models is that they are so adaptable. You can use them to show the formation of RNA from DNA and the formation of protein from RNA. Chains of snap blocks borrowed (with permission) from a younger relative make good models of chains of amino acids. Just changing the color of paper models of DNA adapts them as models for recombinant DNA. Use a different color for each form of life, such as red for the DNA from bacteria, blue for human DNA, and green for DNA from a plant. Putting two bright colors together will give you a vivid illustration of recombinant DNA.

GLOSSARY

adenine (AD-uh-neen)—one of the four bases in DNA and RNA

amino acids—chemical units that are the building blocks of proteins. The order of amino acids in a protein is determined by the order of bases in the mRNA that forms the protein.

anticodon—a group of three bases in tRNA that pairs with a codon in mRNA during the process of protein production

base—one of the chemical substances that make up the "rungs" in the DNA ladder. The information in DNA is contained in the sequence or order of the four different bases.

cap—a base added to the upstream end of RNA during the processing that takes place before mRNA leaves the nucleus

coding region—the part of mRNA that contains codons

codons (KO-dahns)—groups of three bases in mRNA that code for specific amino acids

cytoplasm (SITE-uh-plaz-uhm)—the part of the cell outside the nucleus, where protein production takes place

cytosine (SITE-uh-seen)—one of the four bases in DNA and RNA

deoxyribonucleic (dee-AK-see-ri-boh-nyu-*klee*-ik) acid (DNA)—the chemical substance in the cells of living things that contains the information of life. The information in DNA directs the production of proteins and controls the formation of new cells and of new living beings.

deoxyribose (dee-AK-see-ri-bohs)—a kind of sugar that is one of the two substances in the side pieces of the DNA ladder

enzyme (EN-zime) of transcription—a protein that causes RNA to be transcribed from DNA. The enzyme recognizes the sequence of bases signaling the start of transcription and forms RNA using the base sequence in DNA as a model.

enzymes—proteins that cause chemical changes to take place

gene (JEAN)—a section of DNA that includes the coded message for the amino acid sequence of a single protein

genetic code—the group of 64 codons most of which code for the amino acids used in protein production

genetic engineering—the process of making deliberate changes in DNA. In the future, the products of genetic engineering may be put to use in such fields as medicine, agriculture, and industry.

genetics—the science that studies the information of life contained in DNA

guanine (GWAH-neen)—one of the four bases in DNA and RNA

intervening sequences—sections within the coding regions of DNA and RNA that do not have codons. The intervening sequences in RNA are removed during processing in the nucleus.

leader section—a section at the upstream end of mRNA that lacks codons. The leader section attaches mRNA to the ribosome so that translation will start at the proper spot.

messenger RNA (mRNA)—the form of RNA that carries the coded message of DNA from the cell nucleus to the cytoplasm, where it is used in protein production

mitochondria (mite-eh-KON-dree-uh)—small structures in the cytoplasm of a cell that specialize in energy production

mutation—a permanent change of the information in DNA

nucleosomes (NYU-klee-uh-soms)—structures made up of DNA wound around balls of protein. DNA is packaged in nucleosomes in order to make it fit into the cell nucleus.

nucleus (NYU-klee-uhs)—the information center of the cell, which contains DNA

phosphate (FOS-fate)—one of the two chemical substances that make up the side pieces of the DNA ladder

poly-A tail—a section made up of many adenine bases that is added to the downstream end of mRNA during processing in the nucleus

proteins—complex chemical substances made up of chains of amino acids. Proteins form the structures of cells and perform many functions within them

recombinant DNA—DNA consisting of a combination of bases taken from two different organisms

replication—the process by which the cell copies its DNA in preparation for cell division

ribonucleic (ri-bo-nyu-KLEE-ik) acid (RNA)—a chemical substance formed in the cell nucleus using DNA as a model. Several different forms of RNA play important roles in the production of proteins.

ribose (RI-bose)—the sugar in RNA that takes the place of deoxyribose in DNA

ribosomal (ri-buh-SO-muhl) RNA (rRNA)—a form of RNA found in the ribosomes; rRNA seems to play a role in protein production by helping to hold tRNA in place in the ribosome so that amino acids can be connected together

ribosomes (RI-buh-sohms)—small structures in the cell cytoplasm that serve as centers of protein production

small nuclear RNA (snRNA)—a form of RNA that plays a role in the removal of intervening sequences in mRNA. Unlike other forms of RNA, snRNA does not leave the cell nucleus.

split genes—genes with intervening sequences within their coding regions

thymine (THI-meen)—one of the four bases in DNA. In RNA, thymine is replaced by uracil.

trailer section—a section at the downstream end of mRNA that lacks codons. Scientists do not know the exact function of this part of RNA.

transcription—the process of forming RNA using DNA as a model

transfer RNA (tRNA)—the form of RNA that carries amino acids to the ribosome so that they can be joined together to make proteins

translation—the process of forming a protein by reading the genetic message in mRNA. Translation takes place in the ribosomes and involves several different forms of RNA.

uracil (YUR-ih-sil)—the base in RNA that takes the place of thymine in DNA

INDEX

ACKNOWLEDGMENTS The photographs and illustrations in this book
are reproduced through the courtesy of: p. 6, Control Data Corporation;
pp. 19, 36, 38, 39, Laura Westlund; p. 21, David Prentice; p. 40, Ford
Motor Company; pp. 62, 70, Agricultural Research Service, U.S. Depart-
ment of Agriculture; p. 69, Cetus Corporation.